WHERE'S THE FANCY-DRESS POO?

ORCHARD

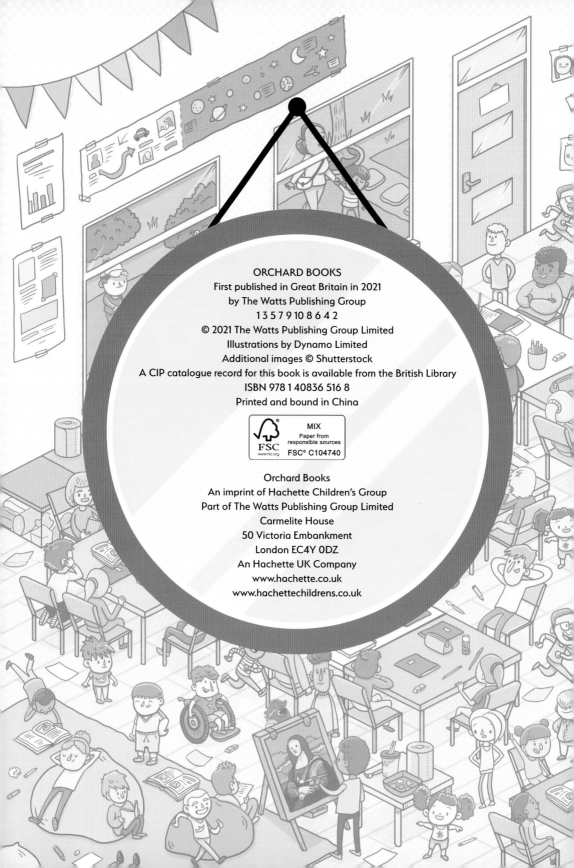

ORCHARD BOOKS
First published in Great Britain in 2021
by The Watts Publishing Group
1 3 5 7 9 10 8 6 4 2
© 2021 The Watts Publishing Group Limited
Illustrations by Dynamo Limited
Additional images © Shutterstock
A CIP catalogue record for this book is available from the British Library
ISBN 978 1 40836 516 8
Printed and bound in China

MIX
Paper from
responsible sources
FSC® C104740
FSC
www.fsc.org

Orchard Books
An imprint of Hachette Children's Group
Part of The Watts Publishing Group Limited
Carmelite House
50 Victoria Embankment
London EC4Y 0DZ
An Hachette UK Company
www.hachette.co.uk
www.hachettechildrens.co.uk

WHERE'S THE
FANCY-DRESS
POO?

MEET THE POOS

It's time to get out the fancy-dress box for this group of poo friends. Spot them hiding throughout the book in their fabulous costumes.

SUPERPOO

It's no surprise that Superpoo wants to dress as a caped crusader – Superpoo to the rescue!

QUEENIE

There's only one costume this royal poo would like – a beautiful, ice-blue princess dress.

BOBBI

As the most adventurous poo, an astronaut's space helmet is the perfect costume for Bobbi.

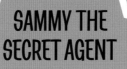

SAMMY THE SECRET AGENT

This poo has mastered the art of blending in. But can you find him in one of the scenes?

DUCKIE

This pirate is heading out to explore the seven seas and make his enemies walk the plank!

ELVIS

What could be cooler than a wise wizard? A wise wizard wearing sunglasses, of course!

FANCY-DRESS ON THE FARM

The fancy-dress poos are making friends at the petting zoo. A cheeky chicken is after Elvis's hat and the hedgehogs are way too close to Duckie's rubber ring!

EAT MY BUBBLES

Superpoo loves swimming almost as much as he loves flying. Find him and the other poos exploring the aquarium.

DRESSED-UP DINERS

After all that swimming, it's time for a snack. Bobbi can't work out how astronauts eat anything while wearing their space helmets. Can you find her?

PIECES OF EIGHT

Duckie has brought his friends to the seaside to look for buried treasure. Where should they dig first? X marks the spot!

LOST IN THE RAINFOREST

The poos are lost deep in the rainforest. Can Elvis cast a magic spell to return them home?

FANCY-DRESS-TIVAL

The dressed-up poos fit right in amongst the painted faces and balloon characters at the music festival. Can you find them all?

WHEELIE GOOD TIME

Elvis's roller-skating skills are magic! Look for him and his friends busting some moves at the roller disco.

PIRATE PLAYTIME

Aarrrr! Captain Duckie and his crew are taking over the waterpark. Spot the swashbuckling poos having fun.

SHARING STORIES

It's story time in class today. Bobbi would like to read a space adventure, while Superpoo chooses a comic with lots of pictures.

POOS IN THE PLAYGROUND

Superpoo is looking out for anyone who needs rescuing from the treetop trail. This hero is always first to help a person (or poo) in distress.

ICE CREAM QUEEN

Queenie has brought the poo friends out for ice cream. She's dressed to impress as an ice princess!

ANSWERS

Now try and find the extra items hidden in each scene.

Did you find me? If you're stuck, try visiting the seaside again.

FANCY-DRESS ON THE FARM

A man in a red top ☐

Nine tortoises ☐

Five peacocks ☐

Three boys wearing caps ☐

Two girls feeding lambs ☐

A green pram ☐

Two hay bales ☐

Two pink roofs ☐

A baby next to a chick ☐

Three goats with purple bells ☐

EAT MY BUBBLES

One angler fish ☐

Two purple puffer fish ☐

Four information screens ☐

A person holding an ice cream ☐

Five starfish ☐

Five prams ☐

Two pairs of sunglasses ☐

Two green octopuses ☐

One swordfish ☐

A girl in a yellow coat ☐

DRESSED-UP DINERS

- Six green stools ☐
- One jukebox ☐
- Two waiters with hot dogs ☐
- A picture of a guitar ☐
- Five people wearing yellow trousers ☐
- Two bottles of mayonnaise ☐
- Ten baskets of fries ☐
- A boy with blue hair ☐
- A lady with a pink headwrap ☐
- A red arrow ☐

PIECES OF EIGHT

- A man with a blue guitar ☐
- Four pink lolly inflatables ☐
- Five dogs ☐
- A crocodile inflatable ☐
- Three cats ☐
- A man holding two ice creams ☐
- Four pineapples ☐
- A starfish balloon ☐
- Eight stripy beach balls ☐
- Two people in kayaks ☐

LOST IN THE RAINFOREST

- Four coiled red snakes ☐
- Four leopards ☐
- Eight blue and yellow macaws ☐
- Nine tigers ☐
- Four sloths ☐
- Eight capybaras ☐
- Six toucans ☐
- Nine giant spiders ☐
- A lady wearing red shorts and hat ☐
- Four flamingos ☐

FANCY-DRESS-TIVAL

Four blue bubbles ☐

Two picnic baskets ☐

Seven panda balloons ☐

Two kids with tiger face paint ☐

A man with a banjo ☐

A person in a frog costume ☐

Two checked picnic blankets ☐

Four birds in a tree ☐

A stripy tent ☐

Four drums ☐

WHEELIE GOOD TIME

A pink fluttering flag ☐

A boy in an orange cap ☐

Three yellow roller-skates on shelves ☐

Nine people who've fallen over ☐

A red and yellow striped jumper ☐

A girl with very long brown hair ☐

A person wearing purple headphones ☐

A child sitting, holding a drink ☐

Two painted roller-skates ☐

A red and white pole ☐

PIRATE PLAYTIME

Two pizza inflatables ☐

Three water slides ☐

Six striped umbrellas ☐

Four starfish ☐

Three people holding ice creams ☐

Two showers ☐

Two inflatable toucans ☐

Three red flags ☐

A child with a heart on their T-shirt ☐

Four people in swimming caps ☐

SHARING STORIES

Eight rolls of blue paper ☐

A globe ☐

Eleven purple books ☐

An orange beanbag ☐

A green pencil case ☐

A pigeon ☐

Four people painting ☐

A teacher in a pink shirt ☐

Four white tables ☐

A girl in green trousers with a satchel ☐

POOS IN THE PLAYGROUND

One green slide ☐

One red seesaw ☐

Three purple dinosaur rides ☐

Five tyres ☐

A boy in a yellow cap ☐

Two white birds ☐

Three dogs ☐

A bucket and spade ☐

A frog ☐

A rabbit ☐

ICE CREAM QUEEN

A purple table ☐

Two green bins ☐

Someone standing on a stool ☐

One dropped ice lolly ☐

A baby hugging a giant ice cream ☐

A lady holding a blue cup ☐

Three glasses on a tray ☐

Two people serving ice cream ☐

A boy on crutches ☐

An old lady licking her ice cream ☐

LOOK OUT FOR MORE POOP-TASTIC BOOKS IN THIS RANGE:

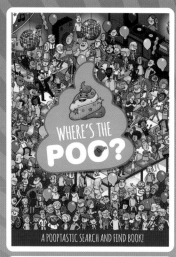

WHERE'S THE POO?

A POOPTASTIC SEARCH AND FIND BOOK!

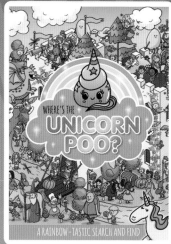

WHERE'S THE UNICORN POO?

A RAINBOW-TASTIC SEARCH AND FIND

WHERE'S THE DINOSAUR POO?

A DINO-TASTIC SEARCH AND FIND

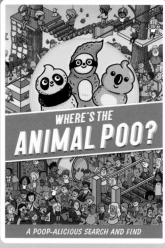

WHERE'S THE ANIMAL POO?

A POOP-ALICIOUS SEARCH AND FIND

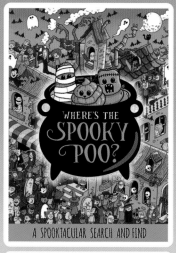

WHERE'S THE SPOOKY POO?

A SPOOKTACULAR SEARCH AND FIND

WHERE'S THE TOILET ROLL?

A POO-PACKED SEARCH AND FIND

WHERE'S THE POO? STICKER ACTIVITY BOOK

OVER 200 POOP-TASTIC STICKERS